The Art of Meditation

A Daily Devotional

Kimberly Moses

Copyright © 2019 by Kimberly Moses

All rights reserved. No part of this publication may be reproduced by any means, graphics, electronic, or mechanical, including photocopying, recording, taping, or by any information storage retrieval system without the written permission of the publisher except in the case of brief quotations embodied in critical articles and reviews.

Kimberly Moses/Rejoice Essential Publishing
PO BOX 512
Effingham, SC 29541

www.republishing.org

Unless otherwise indicated, scripture is taken from the King James Version.

The Art of Meditation/ Kimberly Moses

ISBN-10: 1-946756-62-8
ISBN-13: 978-1-946756-62-6
Library of Congress Control Number: 2019946763

Dedication

This book wouldn't be possible without the inspiration of the Holy Spirit. This manuscript sat in my spirit for many years as the Lord downloaded it to me. He gave me the blueprint and I just obeyed as I wrote the manuscript.

2 Timothy 3:16-17 says, "All scripture is given by inspiration of God, and is profitable for doctrine, for reproof, for correction, for instruction in righteousness: That the man of God may be perfect, thoroughly furnished unto all good works."

Table of Contents

ACKNOWLEDGMENTS...................................xi

CHAPTER ONE: What is Meditation?..........1

CHAPTER TWO: My Testimony.............5

CHAPTER THREE: How To Meditate............11

CHAPTER FOUR: Benefits...............23

CHAPTER FIVE: Prayers................34

CHAPTER SIX: Devotion One:....42

CHAPTER SEVEN: Devotion Two.....45

CHAPTER EIGHT: Devotion Three..................48

CHAPTER NINE: Devotion Four,,...51

CHAPTER TEN:	Devotion Five.....54
CHAPTER ELEVEN:	Devotion Six.......57
CHAPTER TWELVE:	Devotion Seven..................60
CHAPTER THIRTEEN:	Devotion Eight..................63
CHAPTER FOURTEEN:	Devotion Nine....................66
CHAPTER FIFTEEN:	Devotion Ten......69
CHAPTER SIXTEEN:	Devotion Eleven.................72
CHAPTER SEVENTEEN:	Devotion Twelve................75
CHAPTER EIGHTEEN:	Devotion Thirteen.............78

CHAPTER NINETEEN:	Devotion Fourteen.............81
CHAPTER TWENTY:	Devotion Fifteen................84

ABOUT THE AUTHOR...................................87

REFERENCE..90

Acknowledgments

To Tron Moses, thank you so much for being my biggest supporter. You help me to grow and not settle with mediocrity.

To the Millage's, Bonaparte's, Tinker's, and Cunningham's, I love you and appreciate all the support over the years.

To the Edmonds, thank you for all the prayers and support. Good people are hard to find in ministry. I'm glad that I can just be myself around you guys.

To LaShana Lloyd, thank you for traveling with me and praying for me. I appreciate your faithfulness behind the scenes.

To Yolanda Samuels, thank you so much for helping me proofread this book. I love what God is doing through you. Keep going.

CHAPTER ONE

What is Meditation?

Many religions (Hinduism, Buddhism, Judaism, Christianity, Islam, and others) practice meditation. Yoga and Zen also use meditation techniques. Christians should not practice these forms of exercise because it can open up your spirit to the demonic realm. This book is solely focusing on Christianity and how we can draw closer to our Lord and Savior Jesus Christ. Merriam Webster defines 'meditate' as to engage in contemplation or reflection. Some synonyms for meditation are chew over, cogitate, consider, contemplate, debate, deliberate, entertain, eye, kick around, mull (over), perpend, ponder, pore (over), question, revolve, ruminate, study, think (about or over), turn, weigh, and to wrestle (with). We want to focus on Jesus Christ and the goodness of the Lord. We don't want to focus on another deity or things that will grieve the Holy Spirit. Remember, God is a jealous God (Exodus 34:14), and He will share His Glory with no one (Isaiah 42:8).

Some people don't realize how powerful meditation truly is and automatically associate it with something demonic. They get scared of things that they aren't familiar with, or don't quite understand. We have to be cautious about calling things that we don't understand demonic because it could be the Holy Spirit. God allows signs and wonders to follow His servants to prove that He is real (John 4:48; 2 Corinthians 12:12). I have witnessed some people call certain manifestations of the Holy Spirit demonic such as angel feathers (Psalm 91:4), gemstones (Ezekiel 28:13), gold dust (Job 22:24-25), prophecy, and tongues (1

Corinthians 12:8-10), but all these things are Biblical. A sign occurs to point you to Jesus. If a sign manifests and it points you to another deity, then it's demonic. The same concept applies to meditation, which is Biblical. Just because the enemy has used what God has created and tainted it doesn't mean it's not Biblical or that we can't use it today. The enemy is a counterfeit and loves to copy moves of God to deceive people (Exodus 7:8-13). The devil wants us to be deceived and ignorant of his devices (2 Corinthians 2:11). Anything that will help you grow spiritually in Jesus, the enemy will try his best to pervert it.

Ryan Lestrange said several keys things about meditation in His book, "Supernatural Access: Removing Roadblocks in Order to Hear God and Receive Revelation."

Meditation is the digestive system of the kingdom. Meditation is not about twisting yourself into a knot and assuming a physical position like some people do while practicing a false religion. Meditation has little to do with your body and much to do with your mind and spirit. Meditation will help you break down God's wisdom into bite-sized nuggets.

Meditation is for today, and it's an art that needs to be practiced. It's an art because it takes time to develop your skill set. In other words, it takes the training of your mind and your spirit man not to panic but instead remembering the Word of the Lord when conflict arises or facing various challenges. The more you do it, the better you become. Imagine painting a complex picture for the first time. You may not be very good, but the more you paint, you will develop better techniques. God wants us to develop the art form of meditation. I will show you how I started meditating on God's Word. Lastly, we will discover some powerful benefits and how to meditate.

CHAPTER TWO

My Testimony

2013 to 2017 were some of the toughest years of my life. I consider these years my wilderness season because I was living in Colorado Springs, Colorado. Colorado is a beautiful place, and I enjoyed viewing the mountains every day. The temperature is around 77 degrees in the summertime, and I found myself wearing long sleeves year round. It was great seeing the mountain peaks covered in snow most of the year. Even though I was living in a beautiful place, I was suffering. I had gone through a horrible divorce and downgraded my lifestyle. I was crying every day and went from living in a five bedroom house to a one bedroom apartment.

My apartment complex wasn't located in the best area, but it was affordable. As a single parent at the time, I didn't want to overwhelm myself financially. The neighbors were loud sometimes as they got drunk, and they would fight. The police were no strangers to the complex as they would often make arrests. The hallway smelled like weed. I believe that one of my neighbors had a meth lab in his apartment because I caught a glimpse of the black tents and pipes in his living room as I walked by the door of his apartment that was slightly open. Ants infested my apartment complex. I couldn't place the trash bag on the floor the night before and take it out in the morning because if I did, the trash bag would be full of ants as they would eat many holes throughout it. If I sat an ice cream lid on the floor, in two minutes, it would be covered in ants. It was as if the ants could smell food. I was afraid to lay on the floor to pray because bugs, ants, beetles, spiders, or centipedes would crawl on me.

To make matters worse, the apartment complex began to have mice. I saw several of them and the traps I set never worked. I was afraid to sleep with the lights off at times because I was shaken up. I was at my breaking point. I was miserable. The only way I was able to recover from heartache and stress was to cry out to the Lord so I could receive comfort and peace. I was in a dry land, meaning no matter how much I sowed, prayed, fasted, and believed for a turnaround, I was still stuck in my situation. I had to face the facts. I wasn't going back home to North Carolina for a while, which was the place I was familiar with. I was uncomfortable, and I couldn't go back to the east coast until I finished serving two years of probation. How did someone who had it all lose everything? It was due to the bad mistakes that I had made. The Holy Spirit was calling me, but I choose to ignore His voice and sin against Him. I was reaping the adverse consequences of my actions.

During this time, I sought the Lord intensely. I began to have many visitations from Jesus about my assignment in life. Also, I had supernatural encounters with God, and I learned how to flow with the Holy Spirit. The wilderness was my training ground. It was the school of the Spirit for me because I discovered who I was in the Lord. I was praying for hours and praying for others, as the Lord directed me to start a prayer ministry. I would prophesy to everyone that I could because the gift of prophecy was activated and freshly imparted unto me. I fasted weekly because the Holy Spirit gave me instructions to do so. I read the Bible daily because the Lord was calling me to preach the gospel. I worshiped the Lord throughout the day because I enjoyed feeling His fiery presence across my skin. I attended church every time it opened. I thought that I was doing everything that I needed to grow spiritually, but I was wrong.

One day I was washing dishes, and the Holy Spirit spoke to me. "You lost the art of meditation!" I said, "What?" "You lost the art of meditation! You don't meditate on my Word!" Immediately, my heart was filled with conviction as I thought, "Wow. I don't meditate." I said, "Ok, God. You're right. I will start to meditate." As I finished washing the dishes, I pulled out my Bible. I looked at all the Scriptures and started to feel overwhelmed because I thought that I had to meditate on the whole chapter. That's not what the Holy Spirit wanted me to do. He led me to go over one Scripture at a time.

Some days, I spent a couple of minutes or hours meditating on Scriptures. It just depended on my schedule and how long I was able to invest. When I first started, the Lord quickly proved that His Word is alive.

Hebrews 4:12 (EXB) says, "[For] God's word is alive and working [active; powerful; effective] and is sharper than a double-edged sword. It cuts all the way into us, where the soul and the spirit are joined, to the center of our joints and bones [penetrates until it divides even soul and spirit, joints and marrow]. And it ·judges [discerns] the ·thoughts [ideas] and ·feelings [attitudes; intentions] in our hearts."

Something supernatural occurred each time I would meditate. The presence of God would come into my room so strong that I would sweat and tremble. I didn't pray, worship or praise to get His Glory to manifest. All I did was meditate, which was a sign that I was in alignment with what God wanted me to do, and He was pleased with my actions. Over time, I noticed that my prophetic flow increased and my prayer life was strengthened. I was able to prophesy over people five to ten minutes straight as the Holy Spirit would reveal one piece of the puzzle at a time. I was able to pray out the Scriptures I meditated on previously as the Holy Spirit brought His word to my remembrance. Meditation was the missing key that I needed to grow spiritually. Meditation helped me stay sane in the rough environment that I was living in. Let's discuss how to meditate and some of its benefits.

CHAPTER THREE

How to Meditate

1. Make Time

Psalm 90:12 says, "So teach us to number our days, that we may apply our hearts unto wisdom."

Time is valuable, and it's something that you can't get back so make the most of it. Many people don't set time to meditate on the Word of God. You make time for what's important. If you were dating someone, you would make time for them. Regardless of how busy your schedule is, you find the time to text or make a phone call. If you are in a relationship with someone, then you have to make time for them to show them that they are essential in your life. If you don't, then they will get upset and feel like you don't want them to be a part of your life. The same principle applies to the Word of God.

Since my schedule is sometimes hectic, I have to make time to meditate. My time is early in the morning before I start my day or late at night when everyone in my household is asleep. When you meditate, you don't want to rush because you will begin to feel stressed. You don't want any distractions because you aren't able to focus on Scripture. Show the Lord that you are serious about getting His Word deep within your heart by making time.

- When is a good time for you to meditate?
- How long are you able to meditate?
- How much do you want to grow spiritually?

2. One Scripture at a Time

James 1:4 says, "But let patience have her perfect work, that ye may be perfect and entire, wanting nothing."

Have you ever read the Bible in large amounts and not remember what you read? This happens to all of us. I have met and prayed for a lot of people who are discouraged when it comes to meditating on Bible verses. Don't feel bad. Be patient because you will learn how to meditate effectively. I discovered that it's better to read a couple of chapters instead of trying to read an entire book. For instance, I can retain more by reading chapters one and two of the books of Isaiah instead of reading all sixty six chapters in one sitting. Sometimes less is more. I'd rather meditate on one Scripture and master it then meditate on five Scriptures and not get anything accomplished. By meditating on one Scripture at a time, it will be easier for you to remember it.

- What Scriptures will you meditate on first?

- Do you have a plan in place for the Scriptures that you will meditate on?
- What will you do if you start to feel frustrated during the meditating process?

3. Repeat It

Proverbs 24:16 says, "For a just man falleth seven times, and riseth up again: but the wicked shall fall into mischief."

Children of God must never quit. They need to know that they are victorious. If they fall seven times, then they can expect to rise an eighth time. Even when it gets tough, we have to be determined to see it through. This concept applies to meditation because we won't memorize the Scripture the first time we go over it. Often, it requires us going over the same verse again. Repeating the Scripture multiple times is required, especially if you desire to grow spiritually.

For instance, you can read the Bible from Genesis to Revelation many times. However, each time you will see or gain something that you have never seen before. The more you repeat this verse over again in your mind, the more it will stick. Sometimes, it takes me repeating a verse about ten times before I can say it without looking at it.

- Are you willing to work hard to get the Word of God in your heart?
- What do you do when it gets tough?
- Are you willing to repeat the Scripture every day and multiple times throughout the day until you memorize it?

4. Reflect on it

Psalm 119:97 says, "O how love I thy law! it is my meditation all the day."

As you meditate, you have to break the Scripture down on what it means to you. Meditating is like a cow eating, regurgitating, and re-eating. We must go over a verse then ponder upon it. We must ask ourselves, "What does God want me to know about this Scripture?" "Who was this verse written for?" "What is the background of this scripture?" These are some questions that we can ask as we reflect on Bible verses. Meditation is also like a simmering pot of sauce. The longer it simmers, the more flavorful the sauce will be. The longer we ponder on the Word of God, the more we can pull out of the verse, and the more the Word can get into our hearts. Many of my devotional books consist of me reflecting on what the Scripture is saying to me. Reflecting on God's Word is powerful and transformational.

- What is God saying to you as you meditate on the verse?
- Is there a particular word that stands out in the verse?
- How can you apply this verse to your life?

5. Speak it

John 6:63 says, "It is the spirit that quickeneth; the flesh profiteth nothing: the words that I speak unto you, they are spirit, and they are life."

Imagine how your atmosphere will shift as you speak the Word of God. God's Words are Spirit and life. You could be in a faithless environment,

The Art of Meditation

but as you put the Word of God in your atmosphere, it will eventually become faith-filled. His Word is alive so as you meditate, proclaim the Word out of your mouth. You need to hear yourself speaking the Word of God, and the angels (Psalm 103:20) that are assigned to your life need to hear it as well. Speaking the Word of God builds your faith and gives your angels an assignment.

Over time, you will notice that you are talking differently or speaking the way God speaks. When you are speaking out the Word as you go over it, you are actually praying. So you are doing two things at once and being more effective. As I meditate, I say the verse out loud, so I don't look at the Bible. As I hear myself speak out the Scripture, I can tell when I have it memorized or whether I need to continue repeating the verse. If you can no longer read the verse over again, try speaking it out loud.

- Do you have a quiet place that you can go to meditate on the Word of God?
- How can proclaiming the Word of God shift your atmosphere?

- How are you more effective in meditating by speaking Scripture?

6. Pray for Understanding

Jeremiah 33:3 says, "Call unto me, and I will answer thee, and show thee great and mighty things, which thou knowest not."

God desires for us to grow and to come into the knowledge of His glory (Habakkuk 2:14). Before you begin to meditate on Scripture, pray, "Lord, give me an understanding of Your Word." This simple prayer can supernaturally open your spiritual senses and remove spiritual dullness. It also eliminates distractions and resistance that will prevent you from getting what you need from God. The Holy Spirit is our Helper (John 14:26), and we have to learn how to partner with Him.

Many times, I stop and pray before I minister, write, sing, and start my day because I want to be productive. I desire for God to show me great things that I never saw before so I can go to a higher dimension. When I pray for revelation, the Lord blesses me with a Rhema Word, a right now word, or a fresh Word for my season. God is waiting on you to pray for understanding so He can supernaturally open up His Word to you.

- Why is it important to pray for understanding?
- Do you have to have a title or be in a certain position for God to give you a revelation of His word?
- Stop and pray for understanding. Meditate. What were the results?

7. Write It

Revelation 21:5 says, "And he that sat upon the throne said, Behold, I make all things new. And he said unto me, Write: for these words are true and faithful."

Writing the Word of God is a practice that has been used since the beginning of time. I have discovered that writing Scripture repeatedly makes it stick. I purchased a few composition books, and I filled up the notebooks with different Scriptures. Amazingly, the verses always come back to my remembrance as I pray or minister to someone.

I also recommend to every student of mine to write in their composition books the Word of the Lord, which includes Scriptures. Writing is time-consuming, and many people aren't willing to put forth the effort. It's hard work, but the results are worth it. For instance, I discovered that writing books, instead of speaking through voice text apps, help me retain the information better. I tried a couple of speaking apps to help me write books, but sitting down and typing proved to help the most. In other words, writing books took hard work, and meditation takes hard work. However, the results will be worth it when there is an increased flow of the Holy Spirit in your life.

- How can writing down Scriptures help you meditate?
- Do you have any compositions books that you can use?
- What are some Scriptures that you can write down that you would like to meditate on?

8. Keep Track

Jeremiah 30:2 says, "Thus speaketh the Lord God of Israel, saying, Write thee all the words that I have spoken unto thee in a book."

Now that we have discussed writing down the Scriptures that we meditate on in a composition book, let's talk about keeping track of the books. God also spoke to His servants so they could record important events in history, which allows us to witness what happened in that era. For instance, we can gain insight into the many miracles of Jesus and other prophets because it was recorded. From time to time, you want to go back and pick up the books of the previous Scriptures that you have meditated on and go over them again. I have many journals that are full of Scriptures and prophecies that the Lord has given me. I read it and encourage myself. Miraculously, everything that I have written down is in my memory bank, and the Holy Spirit brings it back to my remembrance to use at the right time.

- Why is recording what the Lord has spoken necessary?

- Do you still remember the verses that you meditated on previously?
- How often will you revisit these old notebooks?

CHAPTER FOUR

Benefits

1. The Word is Embedded in Your Heart

Psalm 119:11 says, "Thy word have I hid in mine heart, that I might not sin against thee."

David said in the above psalm that he hid the Word of God in his heart so he wouldn't sin against God. The more you meditate, the deeper the Word of God is in your heart. For instance, when I was single, being pure wasn't as hard because everytime temptation came before me, a

Scripture about holiness would come back to my remembrance. All the scriptures that I meditated on previously about abstinence, fornication, and adultery all came back when I was dealing with temptation. I can testify that I did not sin against God in the time of trying and testing.

Many people read the Bible but when you meditate, you get the Word of God in your heart. When you read the Bible you're reading large amounts of passages at once. When you meditate, you are taking a Scriptures and pondering about it. Therefore, you are taking time by breaking down each Scripture and the Holy Spirit has time to speak to you. You can pull more out of the Scripture. Over time, the Word of God will get in your heart. You will be amazed at how you will begin to learn Bible verses. You will also memorize so many Scriptures.

At the right time, the Holy Spirit will bring every word back into remembrance so you can be more effective in ministering to others. Meditation is putting the Word of God into your Spirit man. You are actually feeding the Holy

Spirit with His Word. His word is getting deep in your heart to bring the transformation process.

2. Drawing Closer to God

James 4:8 says, "Draw nigh to God, and he will draw nigh to you. Cleanse your hands, ye sinners; and purify your hearts, ye double minded."

As you meditate on the Word of God, you are positioning yourself to draw closer to the Lord. As you draw closer to God, then He will draw closer to you. God sees those who are hungering and thirsting after Him. He will then fill them with His righteousness (Matthew 5:6). Meditating on the Word of God will satisfy our hunger for the Lord. Jesus said, "Man shall not live by bread alone, but by every word that proceedeth out of the mouth of God (Matthew 4:4)." Which means our Spirit man needs the Word of God to sustain it, not just physical food. Whatever you put inside of you will eventually come out.

For instance, if you watch drama all day on television, then you might start to fight, curse people out, lust, cheat, steal, and the list continues.

However, if you watch preaching on YouTube all day, then your mind might be on the things of God. As your mind is on the things of God, you are drawing closer to Him. Pondering on God's Word and allowing it to enter into your heart is an open invitation for the Lord to fellowship with you on a deeper level. As I stated earlier, I started to feel the presence of God intensely as I meditated on His Word. The Lord was drawing closer to me because I took steps to draw closer to Him.

3. Think Like the Lord

Proverbs 23:7 says, "For as he thinketh in his heart, so is he: Eat and drink, saith he to thee; but his heart is not with thee."

You will be amazed at how your perspective changes as you meditate on the Lord. You will no longer see things negatively, but you will see the hand of the Lord moving. You will see your circumstances through the lenses of faith. For instance, you may be going through intense warfare, but you will think, "What was meant for evil is working out for my good," "Nothing is too hard for God," "Everything is working out for my good," "I'm more than a conqueror," "I'm victorious," "I'm an overcomer," or "A major door is about to open due to the intense amount of spiritual attacks." You can think on this magnitude because you put the Word of God in your heart and the Holy Spirit is using it to encourage you during the trials. Your faith will increase, and you will live a miraculous life because you're thinking the way Jesus would think. Through many trials, my faith has grown, and my thoughts lined up with the Word of God. The result is a blessed and supernatural life.

4. Becoming a Student of the Word

2 Timothy 2:15 says, "Study to shew thyself approved unto God, a workman that needeth not to be ashamed, rightly dividing the word of truth."

When you meditate on the Word of God, you are breaking it down and gaining a greater understanding. You might be looking up words in the thesaurus to find synonyms. Perhaps you are looking up the definition in the dictionary. Maybe you might look certain words up in Hebrew or

Greek. As you are studying the Word, you might reflect on a particular verse and find out when it was authored, who it was authored by, and look at the geology of the land. As you meditate on the Word of God, you may highlight passages, make sticky notes, or fold pages. The point is that meditation will make you a theologian of the Word.

The enemy knows the Word, which we can see clearly in Luke 4, so children of God need to know it as well. The enemy will use the Word of God to pervert it so children of God must know what the Scripture means. Meditate to show the Lord that you will work hard to grow spiritually. Prove to the Lord that you are serious about your call. Once the Lord spoke to me. He said, "Study my Word like you did when you were getting your Biology Degree." When He spoke these words, I became convicted and a student of the Word of God.

5. Brings Deliverance

Psalm 107:20 says, "He sent his word, and healed them, and delivered them from their destructions."

I had anxiety for five years, and it was debilitating. It was challenging to be around people, and it caused me to have lots of digestive issues. At first, I tried medication, but as it began to wear off, I felt worse than I did before I took the drug. I couldn't function effectively in life, so I decided to try things God's way. I researched anxiety and fear in the Bible. I wrote them down and meditated on them. Whenever I started to feel a panic attack come upon me as I was working, driving, or eating, I would stop and think about the Bible verses on fear. Amazingly, the verses worked, and the fear left. The Word of God brought me deliverance in my mind that medication could never do. What is your issue? Research the Scriptures, meditate, and watch how powerful your deliverance will be.

6. Memorizing Scripture

Psalm 37:31 says, "The law of his God is in his heart; none of his steps shall slide."

Meditating is a powerful way to memorize Scripture. Once, I saw a Facebook status about a

112-year-old lady with dementia who could still recite Bible verses. In the natural, her memory is gone, so there is no way she should be able to quote Scriptures. However, this is a supernatural occurrence because the Word of God is coming from her spirit, not her mind. That's why she can recite Bible verses with dementia.

I have interviewed many ministers for Rejoice Essential Magazine that have testified that they still know all the Bible verses that they had to memorize in Sunday school as a youth. When you train up a child to learn God's Word, those Scriptures are planted inside them (Proverbs 22:6). Meditating on God's Word is supernatural, and verses that you haven't read in years will come back to you because you took the time to memorize them. Go over the Word of God daily so it can become a part of your spirit man.

7. Success

Joshua 1:8 says, "This book of the law shall not depart out of thy mouth; but thou shalt meditate therein day and night, that thou mayest observe to do according to all that is written therein: for then thou shalt make thy way prosperous, and then thou shalt have good success."

Have you ever failed at something? What made you try again, if you did? As believers, when we fail at something, we get back in the race and try it again. Why? Because the Scriptures encourages to fight the good fight of faith (1 Timothy 6:12), press toward the high mark of Christ (Philippians 3:14), endure to the end (Matthew 24:13), that we are overcomers through Christ (John 16:33), and Christ strengthens us (Philippians 4:13). The list continues with the promises of God. The point is that we can't quit no matter how difficult it is because we are destined to win!

When you meditate on the Scriptures, you will be empowered to put your hands to the plow and not look back. Meditation will cause supernatural zeal for the things of God so that you can do great exploits for the Kingdom. As an entrepreneur, I meditate on Scriptures that will elevate my faith to press past the resistance so I can do what the Lord has placed before me. Meditation will bless you with great success.

8. Increase Flow of the Holy Spirit

John 7:38 says, "He that believeth on me, as the scripture hath said, out of his belly shall flow rivers of living water."

Many people ask me often, "How do you increase the flow of the Holy Spirit in your life?" I tell them, "Meditation." The key to an increase in prophetic flow is meditation. When the Lord first started speaking to me, I would hear short phrases, but as I meditated on His Word, I got longer sentences. Sometimes I would hear so much in the Spirit that I would write down pages of prophetic words in my composition books. Whenever someone asks me for prayer, I have no idea what the Holy Spirit will say or do. As I step out in faith into the supernatural flow of the Spirit, I get revelation after revelation. The Holy Spirit will show the person's heart. Then, He will show me their sickness if they are afflicted in their body.

Next, a Scripture will come into my remembrance, and I'll quote it. Afterward, I'm prophesying Scripture after Scripture, or I'm speaking out the images that I see in the realm of the spirit. The flow of the Holy Spirit isn't always in this order, but I learned to flow with Him over time. Before I started meditating, I didn't know how to flow with the Holy Spirit. As I disciplined myself to meditate on the Word of God, His Scriptures flowed out of my belly as living waters (John 7:38).

CHAPTER FIVE

Prayers

I decree that God will keep me in perfect peace because my mind is stayed on Him (Isaiah 26:3).

I decree that I will meditate on the Word of God day and night so I can prosper and have good success (Joshua 1:8).

I decree that whatever is true, whatever is noble, whatever is right, whatever is pure, whatever is lovely, whatever is admirable—if anything is excellent or praiseworthy— I will think about such things (Philippians 4:8).

I decree that I will delight on the law of the Lord and meditate on all His commands (Psalm 1:2).

I decree that my mouth will speak words of wisdom (Psalm 49:3).

I decree that the meditation of my heart shall give me understanding (Psalm 49:3).

May the words of my mouth and the meditation of my heart be pleasing in your sight Lord, my Rock and my Redeemer (Psalm 19:14).

I decree that I will meditate on the Lord during the night watches (Psalm 63:6).

I decree that the meditation of my heart will be pleasing unto the Lord as I rejoice in Him (Psalm 104:34).

I decree that I will meditate on Your precepts and follow Your ways (Psalm 119:15).

I decree that I will not be discouraged but meditate on Your promises (Psalm 119:148).

I decree that I will meditate on the mighty things that You have done before (Psalm 143:5).

Meditation on the Word of God will make me wiser than my enemies (Psalm 119:98).

I decree that meditation on the Word of God will give me more insight than all my teachers (Psalm 119:99).

I decree that I will meditate on Your Word to get to know You more.

I decree that I will meditate on Your Word to know Your ways.

I decree that I will meditate on Your Word to be transformed more in the image of Jesus Christ.

I decree that I will meditate on Your Word as I study to show myself approved unto You.

The Art of Meditation

I decree that I will meditate on Jesus during the storm.

I decree that I will always take time to meditate to get Your Word in my heart, so I don't sin against You.

Lord, please bring back unto my remembrance every Scripture that I meditated on as I witness to the lost.

Lord, bless me to have an increase prophetic flow as I meditate on Your Word.

Lord, bless me to become a great theologian of Your Word.

Lord, bless me to renew my mind every day with Your Word.

Lord, bless Your Word to do a transformative work in my life and those connected to me as I meditate on Your Word.

Lord, increase my revelation of the Scriptures as I meditate on Your Word.

Lord, speak to me as I meditate on Your Word.

Lord, draw me closer to You as I meditate on Your Word.

Lord, stir up the spiritual gifts inside of me as I meditate on Your Word.

Lord, bless me to become more sensitive to Your presence as I meditate on Your Word.

Lord, give me wisdom as I meditate on Your Word.

Lord, give me a great understanding of Your will and agenda in this earth as I meditate on Your Word.

Lord, reveal to me new things in the Scriptures as I meditate.

Lord, bless me to develop the fruits of the Holy Spirit as I meditate on Your Word.

Lord, deliver me from demonic bondage and strongholds as I meditate on Your Word.

Lord, strengthen me as I meditate on Your Word.

Lord, increase my prayer life as I meditate on Your Word.

Lord, bless me to eat and digest Your Word.

Lord, show me how to pray Your Word.

Lord, deepen my love to ponder the Word.

Lord, increase my faith as I meditate on Your Word.

Lord, increase my discernment as I meditate on Your Word.

Lord, bless me to dwell in Your presence as I meditate on Your Word.

Lord, bless me to trust You on a greater dimension as I meditate on Your Word.

Lord, order my steps as I meditate on Your Word.

Lord, bless me to be patient as I meditate on Your Word.

Lord, bless me to walk in a Spirit of Excellence as I meditate on Your Word.

Lord, bless me with favor as I meditate on Your Word.

Lord, bless me to receive healing as I meditate on Your Word.

Lord, bless me to increase in stature as I meditate on Your Word.

Lord, anoint me with boldness as I meditate on Your Word.

Lord, enlighten the eyes of my understanding as I meditate on Your Word.

Lord, bless me to love others as I love myself as I meditate on Your Word.

Lord, bless me to have peace that passes all understanding as I meditate on Your Word.

Lord, deepen my hunger and zeal for You as I meditate on Your Word.

I decree that I have the mind of Christ!

I decree that I will overcome every challenge as I set my mind on the right thoughts!

CHAPTER SIX

Devotion One

Today's Scripture for Meditation: Genesis 24:63 says, "And Isaac went out to meditate in the field at the eventide: and he lifted up his eyes, and saw, and, behold, the camels were coming."

Isaac was the son of Abraham and witnessed the favor of God upon his father's life. He knew that God was his provider because of the ram in the bush experience (Genesis 22:13-14). Isaac was about to receive a mighty prophecy, or promise, from God over his life (Genesis 26:1-5) because he had a heart to meditate as he sought the Lord. Isaac realized the importance of spending time alone with God. He went out to an open field away from everyone. Perhaps, he could view God's creation of nature and enjoy it as he prayed and reflected on the promises of the Lord. Isaac meditated in the evening because he wanted to end his day in prayer. He desired to focus and not be distracted. Imagine how you could touch the heart of the Father by taking time to meditate.

Often, I pulled away from everyone so I can get alone with God. Imagine a busy life as a wife, mother, publisher, CEO of a magazine, mentor, spiritual mother, prophet, intercessor, sister, and daughter! I play many roles, and sometimes, I am pulled in several directions. I purposely shut down my social media accounts for a couple of hours because of the numerous notifications so I can focus on the Lord. Instead of going into the field like Isaac, I go into my car where I can cry, shout, sing, prophesy to myself, and communicate with the Lord. For my sanity, quiet time is a must! I need the Lord to pour back into me everything that I poured out. When I meditate on His promises and who He is, I soak up the Glory!

Do you practice quiet time? Where can you go to meditate on the promises of God?

Dear Heavenly Father,

I repent of my sins. Please forgive me for all the times that I was distracted and neglected Your presence or the unction to pray. Lord, help me to take time out every day to meditate on Your Word, Your promises, and who You are! I decree and declare that I will make the necessary steps to steal away and seek You. I want to grow spiritually and be everything that You are calling me to be. I desire to walk in my purpose and fulfill my assignment on this earth. Thank You, for loving me and never giving up on me in Jesus' name. Amen.

CHAPTER SEVEN

Devotion Two

Today's Scripture for Meditation: Isaiah 26:3 says, "Thou wilt keep him in perfect peace, whose mind is stayed on thee: because he trusteth in thee."

Did you know that during the toughest times in life you can think about Jesus and feel a sense of peace? That's what I had to do many years ago. I was 1,625 miles away from my family, and I was betrayed by someone who I thought would be in my life forever. It felt like I had a knife stuck in my heart, and throughout the day, the pain intensified. I couldn't function because I was an emotional wreck. I would cry all day and lay in bed. When I had to go to work to provide for my family, it was difficult because I had to stop crying and pretend that the pain wasn't there. I remember spending my lunch breaks in the bathroom crying in agony. Something had to change, and that's when I started focusing on Jesus more than I had ever done before.

As I worked twelve-hour shifts, I would whisper underneath my breath, "Jesus, Jesus, Jesus, Jesus." I must've said His name around 10,000 times the first night. I received strength the more I said His name. I was determined not to cry about the betrayal and loss of a relationship. I got up and made up my mind to become the woman God ordained me to be. I stood up and yielded my life to God. Instead of focusing on the pain, I thought about Jesus, who paid the ultimate price for my sins. I started to feel something inside of my heart that I hadn't experienced in a long time. Peace! That's right. I felt the peace of God. I was able to function as a mother and move on in life. Whatever you are going through, meditate on Jesus instead of your pain and watch God give you peace that surpasses all understanding.

Dear Heavenly Father,

I humble myself before You. I repent for thinking the wrong thoughts. I will focus on Your love and promises instead of the disappointments, pain, or injustice that I experienced. I decree and declare that I will focus on Jesus, who is my Source of hope, joy, peace, and strength. I decree and declare that I will not be angry, bitter, depressed, or discouraged by the things that I have suffered. I know that You have an amazing plan for my life, and I will continue to meditate on Your goodness. Thank You for answering this prayer in Jesus' matchless name. Amen.

CHAPTER EIGHT

Devotion Three

Today's Scripture for meditation: Joshua 1:8 says, "This book of the law shall not depart out of thy mouth; but thou shalt meditate therein day and night, that thou mayest observe to do according to all that is written therein: for then thou shalt make thy way prosperous, and then thou shalt have good success."

Everyone in life will face challenging times. During these moments, we might want to quit and walk away from everything or everyone.

However, God's Word encourages us to hold on to the promises and keep on standing in faith. Anything worth having will take hard work and investment. I learned that I appreciate the things that I invested in. With every season in my life, I face a new milestone. I encounter warfare such as demonized people, lack of support or resources, and many distractions, but I have to meditate on the words that the Lord spoke to me and continue on this journey.

Whenever we meditate on the Word of God, we gain strength, and there is a supernatural exchange. Our doubt is replaced by faith in God. Instead of being tempted to give up during the tough times, we press forward. When we reflect on everything that the Word of God says throughout the day and apply it to our lives, we will succeed. Look around. You may be broke right now, but the Word promises wealth. You may be sick right now, but the Word promises good health. You may be waiting on the harvest, but the Word tells us that there is an appointed time that the harvest will come. God desires to bless you. Take a stand today, and take control of your thoughts. Meditate all day so you can have GOOD success.

Dear Heavenly Father,

I exalt You! I will continue to look to You for Your promises are Yes and Amen. I refuse to be bound because You promise freedom. I want to experience Your freedom in a new way. I declare that I will meditate on Your Word so that I will have good success. I prophesy over my destiny as I walk in the Spirit of Excellence, blessings will be magnetized to me. I will forever give You praise in Jesus' name. Amen.

CHAPTER NINE

Devotion Four

Today's Scripture for meditation: Philippians 4:8 says, "Finally, brethren, whatsoever things are true, whatsoever things are honest, whatsoever things are just, whatsoever things are pure, whatsoever things are lovely, whatsoever things are of good report; if there be any virtue, and if there be any praise, think on these things."

What kind of thoughts are running through your mind? Are you consumed by the cares of this life, such as how will you pay your bills? What are you going to eat for dinner? How to become rich and famous? How to get the person you like to notice you? You will be surprised at the many thoughts that run through our minds daily. Some people waste precious time entertaining these ideas, and it leads to sin, loss, and a chaotic life. However, God gives us a strategy for healthy thinking so we can live our best life. When we think on things that are true, honorable, right, pure, beautiful, commendable, morally excellent, and worthy of praise, we will find ourselves succeeding because we refused to allow our minds to be full of negativity.

Growing up into adulthood, I formed many bad habits. One bad habit was to see the negative in everything. I would stress myself out and have panic attacks because I didn't know about faith, hope, or God's promises. I would make assumptions then make hasty decisions that resulted in horrible consequences such as destroying relationships, getting in trouble with the law, and losing my sense of security. One day, I reached my breaking point. I knew that I had to change because I was heading down a path of destruction, and my life was falling apart. I decided to think differently and try things God's way. Over time, I noticed a huge difference in my life. I didn't spend energy plotting revenge or replaying offenses in my mind. I meditated on God's Word and went through a sanctification process. Now, I'm encouraging others to be positive instead of negative. How are you impacting the lives of others around you?

Dear Heavenly Father,

I repent of my sins. Lord, forgive me for the times that I dwelt on negative things that are grievous to You. I decree that I will renew my mind daily and cast down those wicked thoughts. I declare Philippians 4:8 that says, "Finally, brethren, whatsoever things are true, whatsoever things are honest, whatsoever things are just, whatsoever things are pure, whatsoever things are lovely, whatsoever things are of good report; if there be any virtue, and if there be any praise, think on these things." Thank You for answering this prayer in Jesus' name. Amen.

CHAPTER TEN

Devotion Five

Today's Scriptures for Meditation: Psalm 1:1-2 says, "Blessed is the man that walketh not in the counsel of the ungodly, nor standeth in the way of sinners, nor sitteth in the seat of the scornful. But his delight is in the law of the Lord; and in his law doth he meditate day and night."

Many people want to give their input whenever we face challenges. Though the advice seems good, we have to ask ourselves, "Is this advice in the will of God? Is this carnal advice? What would Jesus do in this situation?" For instance, if you are mad with your spouse and vent to an old friend about it, they may tell you to leave instead of praying for your spouse. Another example, if you are having a hard time financially, someone who isn't living for God may pressure you to make fast money such as selling drugs, prostitution, stealing merchandise, stripping, and the list goes on. The Word of God tells us that we are blessed when we don't listen to carnal or sinful advice, but meditate on the Word of God daily so we can build our faith to experience the goodness of the Lord.

Years ago, I was going through a domestic dispute, and my old college friends gave me the worst advice. They told me to fight, destroy everything, and date around. They meant well, but they didn't understand the process that I was going through. I wasn't clubbing anymore, but I was seeking God because He was calling me. I had a deep conviction to do better, so I responded to the call by rededicating my life to Jesus. As I started to read the Bible, Scriptures about love and forgiveness were highlighted to me. I knew my old college buddies were wrong, and Jesus was right. I memorized several verses until I knew them backward and forward. They were deeply embedded in my heart. What kind of counsel are you receiving from the people in your life? Is it in the will of God?

Dear Heavenly Father,

I humble myself. I repent of my sins and wicked thoughts. Create in me a clean heart and renew a steadfast Spirit within me. I don't want to vex Your Spirit by hanging around with people that will draw me away from You. I don't want to listen to sinful advice that will cause me to act foolishly. Lord, touch my mind and revive me in Your Word. Help me get Your Word deep in my heart, so I don't sin against You. Please remove anyone out of my life that is harmful to my spiritual growth. Thank You for answering this prayer in Jesus' name. Amen.

CHAPTER ELEVEN

Devotion Six

Today's Scripture for Meditation: Psalm 19:14 says, "Let the words of my mouth, and the meditation of my heart, be acceptable in thy sight, O Lord, my strength, and my redeemer."

God is omnipresent, which means He is everywhere, and we can't hide anything from Him. He sees the battles that we face in our minds, so it's important that we think thoughts that are pleasing unto Him. God sees our real motives, even though our actions seem pure. He also knows the private conversations that we have. We must realize that we don't belong to ourselves, but Jesus was crucified for us. Once we receive salvation, the enemy will try hard to get us to turn our backs on God. If we aren't yielded to the Holy Spirit and the Word of God, we will act like the world: having no filter on our mouths and indulging in sin. Conversion starts in your heart. Whatever you allow to take root in your heart, will be the thing that you begin to act out. What are you pondering on?

Many years ago, I thought about sex all day long. I would write sexual fantasies down that could've gotten published into books because it was composed of several notebooks. I was a seductress, and I didn't realize how bound I was. I felt like I had to show my body to get attention or steal attention away from another female. I became promiscuous and was trying to find happiness. One day, a man that I was shacking up with took me to church, and I fought back the tears the whole service. God convicted me, which was the start of me accepting Jesus again into my heart, and I disconnected from that sinful relationship. Over several years, I learned not to think about sex all day because sex was the result of lust that I would eventually be delivered from. Instead, I focused on how great God is and the gift of eternal life. If God was to examine your thoughts right now, would He be pleased?

Dear Heavenly Father,

I confess my sins so You can set me free. I don't want to allow the enemy to plant demonic seeds within me. I don't want to go back to the dark place that You delivered me from. Help me to speak words that are edifying to people who hear them. Allow my words to bless You. Purify me with Your refiner's fire so my heart can be pure in Your sight. Burn me up so I can be passionately in love with You. You are my strength and my redeemer. Thank You for answering this prayer in Jesus' name. Amen.

CHAPTER TWELVE

Devotion Seven

Today's Scripture for Meditation: Psalm 49:3 says, "My mouth shall speak of wisdom; and the meditation of my heart shall be of understanding."

Did you know that putting the wrong things inside of you will eventually contaminate you? For instance, if you are binge-watching reality TV shows that are messy, you will eventually start acting and sounding like the people you watch, which was the case with me many years ago. I was defiled in the sight of God, and my language was filthy. Jesus said in Matthew 15:18, "But those things which proceed out of the mouth comes forth from the heart; and they defile the man." In other words, the words that you speak are an indication of what's in your heart. If we meditate, study the Word of God, and read educational textbooks, then our speech will be full of wisdom. What's really in your heart? Can others see the hidden hurts by the words that you speak?

Often, people compliment me about how knowledgeable or wise I am for my age. My strategy is meditating on the right verses and praying to God for wisdom. When God gave me a mandate to start training others in ministry and the prophetic, I had no idea what I was doing. So, I prayed for wisdom and did lots of studying. Eventually, the Lord enlarged my territory and caused my voice to be heard by the right people. The Lord downloaded revelation in my spirit that has been transformational to myself and others. My speech shifted from having a lack of confidence to becoming bold in what the Lord was calling me to do. Are you ready to speak the mysteries of the Kingdom? Take time out daily and think about the Word of God so the Scriptures can flow out as rivers of living water.

Dear Heavenly Father,

Thank You for always being a very present help in the time of trouble. I need You with everything within me. I desire to be a pure vessel unto You. I want my mouth to be full of Your wisdom, so I will take the time to meditate on Your Word. Bless me to have balance and not to be distracted in life. Give me a strategy on how to be more effective when it comes to studying myself unto You. Thank You for answering this prayer in Jesus' name. Amen.

CHAPTER THIRTEEN

Devotion Eight

Today's Scripture for meditation: Psalm 63:6 says, "When I remember thee upon my bed, and meditate on thee in the night watches."

Notice this verse says night watches. There are eight watches in the day, and each are three hours. Night watches are from sunset to sunrise. David must've stayed up all night thinking about the Lord. What a glorious time! One of the best times to meditate is during the night. Our day slows down. Dinner is made, the housework is done, the children are asleep, and now you can have some alone time with the Lord. We aren't distracted by the busyness of the day, but we find ourselves more relaxed. Do you end your day with the Lord? Do you pray before bed or study the Word?

I discovered that I could effectively meditate on God and His Word before I get out of bed. Once I get out of bed, I start my day in prayer. I love to read the Bible instead of watching TV as I end my day. Many times, I read some Scriptures and fall asleep. When this happens, I dream about the Lord or have a God dream that is full of revelation or instructions. I had several encounters with the Lord meditating about Him while lying on my bed. His presence, which feels like fire, engulfs me and goes deep into my bones. Sometimes, I can't move or talk, but I lay still as the tears roll from my eyes because His presence is so intense at times. I encourage myself on all the promises that the Lord has spoken instead of focusing on my current circumstances. Remember to meditate on God throughout the night, especially on the days that you can sleep in. You'll be blessed.

Dear Heavenly Father,

I exalt Your Holy name! I am grateful that I am alive today because I should've been dead. You saved me, and now I can have fellowship with Your Holy Spirit. I decree and declare that I will start and end my day with You. Lord, as I meditate on You, increase my knowledge and understanding of Your Son, Jesus Christ. Download revelation and give me instructions for my next season. Order my steps today. Protect my dreams from the attacks of the enemy and bless me with sweet sleep. Thank You for answering my prayer in Jesus' name. Amen.

CHAPTER FOURTEEN

Devotion Nine

Today's Scripture for Mediation: Psalm 104:34 says, "My meditation of him shall be sweet: I will be glad in the Lord."

What is your perspective of God? Do you view Him as mean, loving, kind, merciful, humorous, etc.? The fact is that God is multifaceted. There are many sides to Him that we must get to know. When I lived in Colorado Springs, I was going through a difficult time. I would often cry because I was battling depression and discouragement. I remember the Holy Spirit would come into my room and comfort me with His fire. Immediately, I received supernatural joy and burst out laughing, which has happened on several occasions. I couldn't believe how fast my countenance shifted. God truly has a sense of humor.

I learned that if God has spoken something to me, then I have to align my faith up with His Word. I proclaim the promises, pray, praise, meditate, and worship. I encourage myself in the Lord. I can't afford to miss out on my blessings by doubting and being double minded. You can't afford it either. The Lord is faithful, and His promises are sure. It's only a matter of time before you receive the manifestation of what you are believing for. Meditate on the goodness of the Lord, and you shall be blessed.

Dear Heavenly Father,

I honor You. I won't fall apart emotionally when things don't go my way. I won't lose hope when it seems as if nothing is happening. I won't give up when things get tough. Lord, strengthen and cover me in Your grace. I need You with everything within me. I decree and declare that I will meditate on all Your attributes. Thank You for answering this prayer in Jesus' name. Amen.

CHAPTER FIFTEEN

Devotion Ten

Today's Scripture for meditation: Psalm 119:15 says, "I will meditate in thy precepts, and have respect unto thy ways."

Did you know that there is more to God than just going to church? We are called to go outside of the walls of the church and spread the good news of the gospel (Matthew 28:16-20). Many people are content with sitting on the pews every week and never advancing in their assignment on their life. You can go as high in God as you want to, which takes discipline, obedience, and sacrifice. God wants to equip us to do His work by anointing us and giving us power through His Spirit to demonstrate His Kingdom. To be effective, we must study to show ourselves approved unto Him (2 Timothy 2:15), and meditate on His Word to get it deep within our hearts.

When God opened the realm of miracles over my life, I was required to study Jesus and the different miracles in the Bible. As I studied the Word, my faith increased, and I was able to overcome every challenge. For instance, a woman called my prayer line once because her fingers on her hand were crooked. The Holy Spirit gave me a word of knowledge, and she came forward. As I prayed for her, the Scriptures about the man with the withered hand that Jesus prayed for came to mind (Mark 3:1-6). I told the lady to stretch forth her hand, and miraculously, the Lord straighten out her fingers, which was so powerful. Immediately, everyone that witnessed the lady's hand being restored began to praise the Lord. Meditating on miracles increased my faith to operate in the miraculous. Are you ready to walk in everything that God has for you? Meditate on His Word to boost your faith.

Dear Heavenly Father,

I honor and bless You. Bless me with strategies to grow spiritually. Give me wisdom on how to study effectively. Lord, remove any distractions that tries to prevent me from studying Your Word. I desire to walk in my purpose and receive everything that You have for me. I know that to whom much is given much more is required. I'm willing to sacrifice by investing prayer, time, fasting, and receiving training so I can be equipped for what you have mandated me to do. Thank You for Your faithfulness in Jesus' name. Amen.

CHAPTER SIXTEEN

Devotion Eleven

Today's Scripture for Meditation: Psalm 119:78 says, "Let the proud be ashamed; for they dealt perversely with me without a cause: but I will meditate in thy precepts."

As you begin to walk in your purpose, there will be all kinds of demonized people that will come against you. They will try to discourage you and say all kinds of evil things about you. Sometimes, they will pray against you or even curse you. Sadly, most of these people aren't

The Art of Meditation

even aware that the devil is using them. Anytime someone goes against the will of God purposely, then that person is false. No matter what they try to do against you, don't get distracted and don't get in your flesh. The enemy wants you to react. David, in the Psalm above, said that he would meditate on the Word of God because his enemies mistreated him for no reason. David knew that he had to get the Word of God in His heart so that he wouldn't retaliate against his enemies. Whenever your mind is full of the Word of God, you will think differently and recognize the enemy that's in operation.

I learned that I could do more damage on my knees in prayer instead of taking matters into my own hands. Many people have tried to take advantage of my kindness. Some people mistreated me for no apparent reason. I went to God about them, He intervened. Unfortunately, some people got sick, or they ended up being shamed publicly. I had to make sure my heart was pure in the sight of God so instead of rejoicing at my enemies' downfall, I prayed earnestly for their healing, blessing, and the mercy of God to cover them. In those moments where I was mistreated, I had to renew my mind and miraculously God gave me peace. Also, He strengthened me. I always tell people to never place themselves on the same level as a demon by arguing with them. As you grow in your relationship with the Holy Spirit, your discernment will increase.

Dear Heavenly Father,

I humbly come before You. Help me to respond the right way when my enemies test me. I crucify this flesh, so I don't get out of character and grieve Your Holy Spirit. Lord, guide me and order my steps. Keep me from evil and protect me from my enemies. Lord, vindicate me and bless me with justice. I forgive anyone who has wronged me. Lord bless them. I decree that I will love my enemies and show them the love of God. Thank You for answering this prayer in Jesus' name. Amen.

CHAPTER SEVENTEEN

Devotion Twelve

Today's Scripture for Meditation: Psalm 143:5 says, "I remember the days of old; I meditate on all thy works; I muse on the work of thy hands."

Whenever you are going through a challenging time, what types of thoughts are racing through your mind? Some people think, "I can't do this," "It's too hard," "I give up," or "No one is ever going to support me!" During these times, when our faith is shaken, we have to tell ourselves, "If God did it before, then He will do it again." It's all about having a history with God. Many of us should be dead, sick, defeated, and the list continues, but God redeemed us. When David authored this psalm, he knew that he had to remember the 'old days' or the past times where God moved. David had to constantly renew his mind so that he wouldn't get discouraged.

During my wilderness season, or the period where I was going through a difficult time for an extended season, I learned to trust God. Before the tribulation, I thought I had faith but quickly discovered that I had a small measure of it that would eventually increase through the trials. For instance, when I got evicted, the Lord blessed me shortly afterward with an apartment that I didn't have to pay rent for the remainder of that year. From that experience on, I meditated on God as my provider, and I never doubted what He could do ever again. We must decide to stand firm in our faith and cast down every thought that is contrary to it.

Dear Heavenly Father,

I give you praise, and I am thankful for all the times that You have shown Yourself strong and mighty. Thank You for being my friend in lonely times. You have never left me nor forsaken me. Thank You for being my provider. You always made sure that I had everything I needed. Thank You for Your mercy because of You, I have another opportunity to experience Your goodness. I decree that I will reflect on the times of old. I decree that I will celebrate others instead of being jealous of them. I know that if You did it for them than You can do it for me because You are no respecter of persons. Thank You for Your saving grace in Jesus' name. Amen.

CHAPTER EIGHTEEN

Devotion Thirteen

Today's Scriptures for Meditation: Psalm 119:97-99 says, "O how love I thy law! it is my meditation all the day. Thou through thy commandments hast made me wiser than mine enemies: for they are ever with me. I have more understanding than all my teachers: for thy testimonies are my meditation."

God is more powerful than the enemy. The enemy may be cunning, but God will make you wiser than your enemies. The enemy loves to intimidate and cause fear in God's people. However, we must realize that God hasn't given us a spirit of fear. Despite the enemy's attacks, we must fight back and continue moving forward in our purpose. God loves to provide us with strategies that are full of wisdom, so we can know how to fight the enemy effectively. David knew that as He meditated on the Word of God, he would gain a deeper revelation of who God is. Also, David would discover who God created him to be.

A person should desire a prophetic anointing. You don't have to be in the office of a prophet to be prophetic. There were times where the Lord revealed the enemy's plans in my life and others. For instance, the Lord showed me that the enemy was planning to kill a young lady by a car accident. I was assigned to pray for this lady's life and her destiny. A couple of weeks later, the car accident happened, but the lady walked away without a scratch. She was perfectly fine, but her car was totaled. It was bent up. She posted photos on social media, giving God praise. The Lord outsmarted the enemy by exposing his plans and raising up intercessors to combat the assignment of hell.

Dear Heavenly Father,

I am grateful for Your protection. You are my deliverer. You cover me underneath Your shadow. You don't allow any of the hairs on my head to be harmed. You cancel the enemy's plans against me. Thank You for Your faithfulness. Lord, bless me with strategies on how to engage in warfare. Lord, place on me the full armor of God that is listed in Ephesians 6. Lord, train my hands to war and my fingers for battle. Lord, make me Your battle ax and Your weapon of war. Lord, shield me and my family from demonic attacks. Lord, expose every demon that's hidden in my life. Thank You for answering this prayer in Jesus' name. Amen.

CHAPTER NINETEEN

Devotion Fourteen

Today's Scripture for Meditation: Psalm 119:11 says, "Thy word have I hid in mine heart, that I might not sin against thee."

Every day we make choices, and we have to decide if we will give into our fleshly desires. Sometimes, our flesh wants to do things that are sinful such as fornication, alcohol, gambling, fighting, and more. David knew that if he took time to meditate and get the Word of God deep within his heart, he would not sin against God because every time he faced temptation, the Holy Spirit would bring the Word back to his remembrance. The more you meditate on God's Word, the more conscious you become of His ways. Once you know His ways, you don't want to sin against Him.

Years ago, I was carnal and didn't know how real God was. I indulged in a sinful lifestyle and backslid. It wasn't until God made Himself real to me that I became aware of His presence and my wicked ways. I repented and vowed to God that I would go all the way with Him. It's been years, and I haven't stopped. One of the things that has kept me Holy is the thought, "My assignment is bigger than me. If I mess up, then so many people will be affected." The idea of sinning and falling astray is terrifying. So I decided to hide the Word of God in my heart, so I would not sin against Him. Do you have the Word of God embedded in your heart?

Dear Heavenly Father,

I repent of my sins. I need you, and I love you. I don't want to sin against you. Deliver me from temptation and protect me against the evil one. Help me to focus on what's truly important, which is Your Son, Jesus Christ. Bless me never to stumble and walk away from You. Bless me to never shame You. Lord, uproot any evil thing out of me and cultivate me in You. Thank You for answering this prayer in Jesus' name. Amen.

CHAPTER TWENTY

Devotion Fifteen

Today's Scripture for Meditation: Psalm 104:34 says, "My meditation of him shall be sweet: I will be glad in the Lord."

In life, we will have good and bad days because it rains on the just and unjust (Matthew 5:45). However, in every moment, we can remain hopeful when we think about the Lord. When we think about the Lord, we can be strengthened in our faith and reassured that everything will be okay. When we go through the river, we will not drown

The Art of Meditation

or be overwhelmed by the trials in life. When we go through the water, the Lord is there to comfort us. When we go through the fire, we will not smell like smoke or look like we went through anything (Isaiah 43:2). This is what meditation does for us.

When others rejected me, I wanted to quit, but the Lord wouldn't allow me. I meditated on Jesus, and my faith was rejuvenated. Afterward, I was ready to jump back in the race. I realized that during the times that I wanted to quit, I had lost focus. My focus was supposed to be on Jesus, but temporarily, I placed it on my desires. I repented and renewed my mind. I am determined to continue in my assignment because I love the Lord and want to please Him. You may be going through the storm, but be glad in the Lord so you can remain steadfast on this journey.

Dear Heavenly Father,

I humble myself. Thank You for sending Your only begotten Son, Jesus Christ, to die for my sins. I am grateful that He is our living atonement. I am grateful that Jesus is the Prince of

Peace. I bind up depression, discouragement, and heaviness in Jesus' name. I decree that I will not be shaken. I decree that I will put on the mind of Christ Jesus. Thank you, Lord, for answering this prayer in Jesus name. Amen.

About The Author

Kimberly Moses started off her ministry as Kimberly Hargraves. She is highly sought after as a prophetic voice, intercessor and prolific author. There is no doubt that she has a global mandate on her life to serve the nations of the world by spreading the Gospel of Jesus Christ. She has a quickly expanding worldwide healing and deliverance ministry. Kimberly Moses wears many hats to fulfill the call God has placed on her life as an entrepreneur over several businesses including her own personal brand Rejoice Essentials which promotes the Gospel of Jesus Christ.

She also serves as a life coach and mentor to many women. She is also the loving mother of two wonderful children. She is married to Tron. Kimberly has dedicated her life to the work of ministry and to serve others under the call God has placed over her life. Kimberly currently resides in South Carolina.

She is a very anointed woman of God who signs, miracles and wonders follow. The miraculous and incessant testimonies attributed to her ministry are incalculable, with many reporting physical and mental healing, financial breakthroughs, debt cancellations and other favorable outcomes. She is known across the globe as a servant who truly labors on behalf of God's people through intercession.

She is the author of The Following:

"Overcoming Difficult Life Experiences with Scriptures and Prayers"
"Overcoming Emotions with Prayers"
"Daily Prayers That Bring Changes"
"In Right Standing,"
"Obedience Is Key,"
"Prayers That Break The Yoke Of The Enemy: A Book Of Declarations,"
"Prayers That Demolish Demonic Strongholds: A Book Of Declarations,"
"Work Smarter. Not Harder. A Book Of Declarations For The Workforce,"
"Set The Captives Free: A Book Of Deliverance."
"Pray More Challenge"
"Walk By Faith: A Daily Devotional"

"Empowering The New Me: Fifty Tips To Becoming A Godly Woman"

"School of the Prophets: A Curriculum For Success"

"8 Keys To Accessing The Supernatural"

"Conquering The Mind: A Daily Devotional"

"Enhancing The Prophetic In You"

"The ABCs of The Prophetic: Prophetic Characteristics"

"Wisdom Is The Principal Thing: A Daily Devotional"

"It Cost Me Everything"

"The Making Of A Prophet: Women Walking in Prophetic Destiny"

You can find more about Kimberly at www.kimberlyhargraves.com

References

Lestrange, Ryan. Supernatural Access: Removing Roadblocks in Order to Hear God and Receive Revelation. Charisma House: Lake Mary, Florida. 2017.

Index

A

atmosphere, 16–17

B

blessings, 67, 73

C

carnal advice, 54
church, 8, 58, 69
countenance, 67

D

decree, 34–37, 41, 44, 47, 53, 68, 74, 77, 86
deity, 2–3
deliverance, 28–29, 88
deliverance ministry, 87
dementia, 30
demon, 74, 80
depression, 86

destiny, 50, 79
digestive system, 3
dimension, 18, 39
discernment, 39
discouragement, 66, 86
distractions, 12, 18, 49, 71
dreams, 64–65

E

enemies, 3, 28, 58–59, 65, 73–74, 79–80, 88

F

faith, 17, 26–27, 32, 39, 49, 52, 55, 67, 70–71, 75–76, 84–85, 88
faithfulness, 71, 80
fear, 29, 79
fellowship, 26, 65
flesh, 73–74
forgive, 44, 53, 74
forgiveness, 55
fornication, 24, 81
freedom, 50

G

Glory, 9, 43
gospel, 8, 87
grace, 67

H

harvest, 49
hasty decisions, 52
heart, 8, 11–12, 15–16, 23–26, 35, 37, 43, 46, 56–61, 70, 73, 82
heartache, 7
Holy, 2, 8, 38, 58, 74, 82

I

instructions, 64–65
intercession, 88
intercessors, 43, 80, 87

J

Jesus, 3, 7, 21, 27, 36, 45–47, 55, 58, 70, 85

K

kingdom, 3, 31, 61

L

life, 5, 7, 12, 16–17, 20, 29, 32, 43, 45–49, 51–53, 55–56, 69–70, 79–80, 84–85, 87
love, 39–40, 47, 59, 64, 74, 83, 85
loving, 44, 66
lust, 25, 59

M

manifestations, 2, 67
medication, 29
mercy, 73, 77
mighty, 18, 36, 77
mind, 3–4, 15, 26, 29–30, 37, 41, 46, 51–53, 56–57, 70, 73–74, 76, 85–86, 89
ministry, 61, 87–88
miracles, 21, 70, 87
miraculous life, 27
mouth, 17, 35, 61–62

P

pain, 46–47
parent, single, 6

peace, 7, 40, 45–47, 74, 86
praise, 9, 51–53, 67, 70, 77
praiseworthy, 35
prayer life, 10, 39
praying, 8, 55, 61
promises, 43–44, 47, 49–50, 52, 64, 67
prophesy, 8, 10, 43, 50
prophetic flow, 10, 32, 37
prophetic words, 32
prophets, 21, 43, 79, 89
prosperous, 31, 48
purify, 25, 59

R

redeemer, 57, 59
resistance, 18, 31
revelation, 3, 14, 18–19, 64, 79

S

sacrifice, 70–71
sanctification process, 53
season, 19, 49, 65
servants, 2, 21
sexual fantasies, 58

sinful advice, 55–56
sins, 7, 23–24, 37, 44, 46, 52–53, 56, 58–59, 81–83
spiritual attacks, 27
spiritual gifts, 38
spiritual growth, 56
success, 31, 34, 48–50, 89
Supernatural, 89
supernatural joy, 67
supernatural life, 27
sweet sleep, 65

T

temptation, 24, 82–83
trials, 27, 76, 85
tribulation, 76

V

voice, 7, 61

W

war, 80
watches, 29, 60, 63

wisdom, 3, 11, 38, 61–62, 71, 79

Y

Yoga, 1

Z

Zen, 1

www.ingramcontent.com/pod-product-compliance
Lightning Source LLC
Chambersburg PA
CBHW050203130526
44591CB00034B/1999